Contents

The weather

There are lots of different types of weather. How much do **YOU** know about the weather?

False?

her

nn

Raintree is an imprint of Capstone Global Library Limited, a company incorporated in England and Wales having its registered office at 7 Pilgrim Street, London, EC4V 6LB – Registered company number: 6695582

www.raintreepublishers.co.uk
myorders@raintreepublishers.co.uk

Text © Capstone Global Library Limited 2013
First published in hardback in 2013
Paperback edition first published in 2014

Edited by Dan Nunn, Rebecca Rissman, and Catherine Veitch
Designed by Joanna Hinton-Malivoire
Picture research by Ruth Blair
Production by Helen McCreath
Originated by Capstone Global Library
Printed and bound in China

ISBN 978 1 406 25159 3 (hardback)
16 15 14 13 12
10 9 8 7 6 5 4 3 2 1

ISBN 978 1 406 25165 4 (paperback)
17 16 15 14
10 9 8 7 6 5 4 3 2 1

British Library Cataloguing in Publication Data
Nunn, Daniel.
Weather. – (True or false?)
551.6-dc23
A full catalogue record for this book is available from the British Library.

Acknowledgements
We would like to thank the following for permission to reproduce photographs: iStockphoto pp. 4 (© Grady Reese), 13 (© luoman), 20 (© Judy Barranco); Shutterstock pp. 4 (© Smit, © Algecireño, © BestPhotoByMonikaGniot), 5 (© Iakov Kalinin, © Alinute Silzeviciute), 6 (© grafvision), 7 (© AISPIX by Image Source, © topora), 8 and back cover (© Valua Vitaly), 9 (© Bas Meelker), 10 (© Anest), 11 and back cover (© Loskutnikov, © cardiae), 12 (© Lars Christensen), 13 (© UgputuLf SS), 14 (© Nazzu), 15 (© Christopher Elwell, © cobalt88), 16 (© WDG Photo), 17 (© Poznyakov), 18 (© Pigprox), 19 (© FWStupidio), 21 (© Pincasso), 22 (© Jhaz Photography).

Cover photographs reproduced with permission of Shutterstock (© Iakov Kalinin (palm tree scene), © Gorilla (snowman)).

Every effort has been made to contact copyright holders of material reproduced in this book. Any omissions will be rectified in subsequent printings if notice is given to the publisher.

What to wear

We wear coats,
hats, and scarves
when the weather
is hot and sunny.

True or false?

✖ False!

We wear coats, hats, and scarves when the weather is cold. The clothes keep us warm!

Sunglasses

We wear sunglasses when the weather is cloudy and gloomy.

✔ **True or** (**or**) **false?** ✘

✗ False!

We wear sunglasses when the weather is sunny. The sunglasses help to protect our eyes from the bright sun.

Snow

Snow is made of frozen water.

✔ True or false? ✗

✔ **True!**

Snow is made of frozen water.
Frozen water is called ice.

Clouds

Clouds are made of cotton wool.

✖ False!

Clouds are not made of cotton wool.
Clouds are made of lots of teeny, tiny
drops of water.

Fog

Fog is made of clouds that are near the ground.

✔ True or false? ✗

13

✔ True!

Fog is made of clouds that are near the ground. It can be difficult to see very far on a foggy day.

Wind

Wind can make your television work!

✓ True!

Wind turbines like these use wind to make electricity. Electricity makes televisions and other gadgets work.

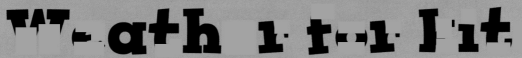

Weather or not?

People fly kites when
the weather is windy.

 True or false?

✓ True!

People fly kites when the weather is windy. If there is no wind, the kites do not fly.

Umbrellas

People use umbrellas to go flying on a windy day.

 True or false?

✖ False!

People do not use umbrellas to fly. People put up umbrellas on a rainy day to keep dry.

Thunder

We hear thunder when an aeroplane flies into a cloud.

 True or false?

✕ False!

Thunder is not made when an aeroplane flies into a cloud. Thunder is the noise made by lightning!

Can you remember?

What keeps us warm when the weather is cold?
What keeps us dry on a rainy day?
What protects our eyes from the bright sun?

Look back through the book to check your answers.

Index

Activity

Make your own True or False game

Help your child to make their own Weather: True or False game. Collect a selection of pictures of the weather from magazines. Mount each picture on card. Then with the child write a series of true or false statements about the weather in the pictures on separate pieces of card. Put one statement with each corresponding picture. On the back of each picture write if the statement is true or false. For the game, read the statement out loud, ask the child if it is true or false, then turn over the picture to see if the child is correct. To extend the activity, ask the child to write the statements and whether they are true or false, and then ask you the questions.